Design IN THE SERVICE OF BEAUTY

Design
IN THE SERVICE OF BEAUTY

AN APPRECIATION OF THE ADVERTISING AND PACKAGING OF BEAUTY PRODUCTS FOR WOMEN

BY WELLERAN POLTARNEES

BLUE LANTERN BOOKS · MCMXCIV

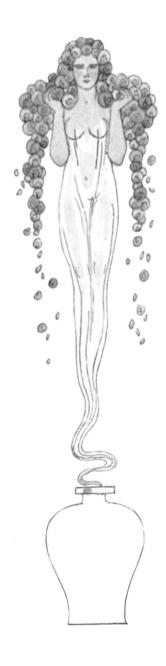

FIRST PRINTING. PRINTED IN HONG KONG THROUGH SOUTH SEAS INTERNATIONAL PRESS.
BOOK & COVER DESIGN BY CHEV DARLING AT BLUE LANTERN STUDIO.
ISBN 0-9621131-8-2

BLUE LANTERN BOOKS
PO BOX 4399 • SEATTLE • WASHINGTON • 98104

*A*lmost all of us wish to be attractive, and we likewise suspect that we are not succeeding. On these twin foundations of hope and fear the cosmetics industry has built an enormous range of beauty products, and, with the help of advertising, has made these seemingly expendable aids into necessities.

My focus in this book is beauty products for women. This subject is vast, and I make no pretense to survey, let alone compass, the field. I have chosen some materials that I find attractive, and from them have attempted to extract a few general truths.

Though the arts of design and persuasion have often been tastelessly used by the advertisers of beauty products, one can admire the talent that has been utilized. The use of psychology is shamelessly manipulative of women's insecurities. Art and design are less despicably involved, and one can enjoy them with only a touch of condescension. I conclude the book with two chapters on the packaging and labeling of beauty products. Here one's appreciation is whole, for art has been allowed to flourish.

IDEALS of BEAUTY

Physical Perfection

That Schoolgirl Complexion

L'AIMANT "THE MAGNET" COTY

The unloved person, of either sex, tends to look on the world's indifference with a mixture of hope and despair. Each is likely to believe that something in themselves must need repair or improvement, since so many others are loved. They face a vast array of possibilities. On the one hand are many, seemingly unchangeable problems – an unattractive personality, bad manners, genetic flaws, a lack of imagination or charm. On the other hand are simpler matters – skin tone, dry hair, body odor, etc. Who would not choose the latter group as the area on which to work?

Pompeian Beauty Powder

The Lure of Beauty

These three for Instant Beauty

Spend all you have for loveliness.
Buy it and never count the cost;
For one white singing hour of peace
Count many a year of strife well lost,
And for a breath of ecstasy,
Give all you have been or could be.

Sara Teasdale

*M*odern industrial society favors youth for many reasons. In it skills passed from generation to generation are of diminishing importance. Innovation substitutes for experience. Strength, endurance and adaptability are necessary in workers – and these traits are most marked in the young. A capitalist market necessitates a public anxious for the new, ready to believe that fresh needs are constantly being born. These production and marketing needs have changed fundamentally the subject of youth and old age.

P. S. Keep That Schoolgirl Complexion

Better than jewels
—that schoolgirl complexion

Inasmuch as the human skin is the the most accurate reflection of age it is natural the makers and users of beauty products should focus on it. Palmolive confronts the matter squarely. It promises it can allow a woman to "keep that schoolgirl complexion." All she has to do is wash her "face gently with Palmolive soap, massaging its balmy lather softly into the skin." They also remind us that "Youth is charm, and youth lost is charm lost." Woodury soap is as direct: "Youth and Love – Keep them by keeping beautiful skin." Pompeian promises that if you will use their three products (vanishing cream, powder and rouge) "The face is beautified and youth-i-fied." They also assure the user that "She will always seem young and girlish to him, she has the secret of instant and permanent beauty." Palmolive, in another ad says "The charm of youthful allure is no longer restricted to youth itself."

YOUTH AS THE STANDARD

The promise of youth permeates beauty advertising. Readers are captured by such headlines as, "Do you look as young as your husband?" or "Fashions Favor a youthful Figure" or "If you lose Youth you lose Beauty!" They are then reassured by promises such as, "Now women grow young – not old." "You can have skin like a baby's: The clean fresh loveliness of youth, which first attracted him, will always be yours."

Helen Woodward, the founder of a large cosmetics firm, in speaking to her force in the early 1920's, was particularly clear in her grasp of the situation. "Remember that what we are selling is not Beauty – it is youth. We are going to sell every artificial thing there is...and above all things it is going to be young – young – young! We make women feel young."

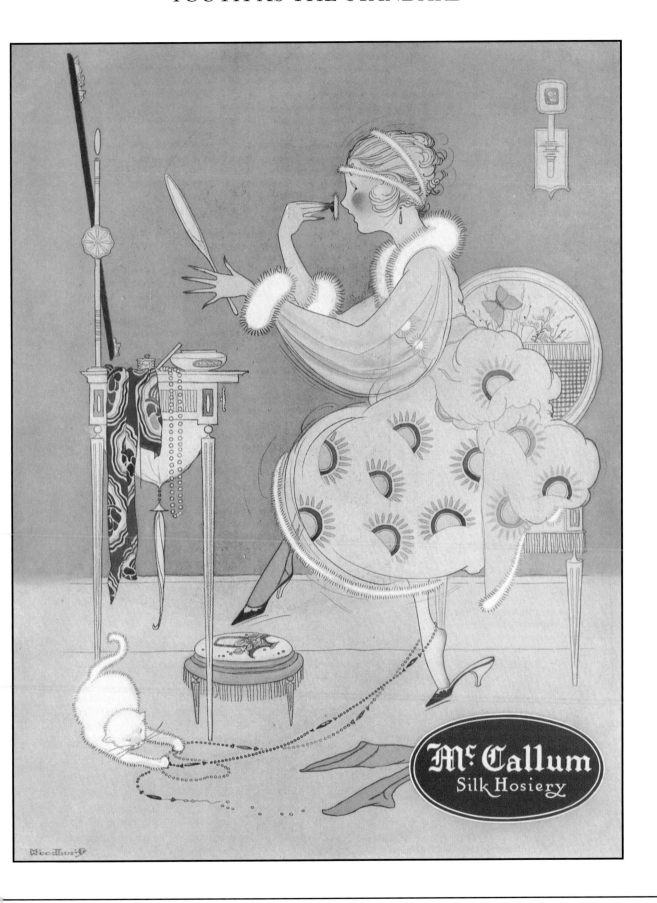

The advertisers would have women believe that their beauty is under constant scrutiny and continual threat. Lady Esther Face Cream says "Men's eyes are magnifying mirrors." Camay soap says, "The eyes of men, the eyes of women, judge your beauty each day." Sage and Sulphur lotion asks, "are you keeping up with other women?" Mme Jeannette, Specialiste en Beauté, counsels "When you neglect to care for your skin, you run the risk of being neglected yourself." Camay sees the drama this way: "Every day of a girl's life means a new Beauty Contest."

Do You Carry "Beauty Insurance"

Is your beauty protected—are you insuring your attractiveness and charm

Beauty is Youth at all Ages

Thousands have retained it in this gentle, natural way

NOTE how conspicuously absent is the "middle-aged" woman in the modern social scheme. Note how the charm of youthful allure is no longer restricted to Youth itself . . .

That is because artificial beauty methods have given way to a more gentle, natural method—and thus youthful charm through the thirties, and even well past the forties, is the custom of the day.

Beauty is retained through the years, safeguarded by *gentle and natural* ways in skin care. Only the woman who has lost the lure of youth, through improper care, knows how true this is.

The accepted rule in skin care today is . . . daily cleansing of skin and pores with the balmy lather of Palmolive.

Do this for one week. Note the difference in your skin

Wash your face gently with soothing Palmolive. Then massage it softly into the skin. Rinse thoroughly. Then repeat both washing and rinsing. If your skin is inclined to be dry, apply a touch of good cold cream—that is all. Do this regularly, and particularly in the evening.

Use powder and rouge if you wish. But never leave them on over night. They clog the pores, often enlarge them. Blackheads and disfigurements often follow. They must be washed away.

Avoid this mistake

Do not use ordinary soaps in the treatment given above. Do not think any green soap, or represented as of olive and palm oils, is the same as Palmolive.

And it costs but 10c the cake—so little that millions let it do for their bodies what it does for their faces. Obtain a cake today. Then note what an amazing difference one week makes.

THE PALMOLIVE COMPANY (Del. Corp.), CHICAGO, ILLINOIS

Palmolive Soap is untouched by human hands until you break the wrapper—it is never sold unwrapped

3031

VIGILANCE IS THE PRICE OF BEAUTY

Woman, according to the advertisers, not only needs to relentlessly protect her beauty from erosion, she must also guard against lurking perils, especially body odor. Odo-Rono tells us, "A man cannot forgive this deadly little sin. A woman may have a crooked nose or muddy skin – and she can still be so charming that men will fall in love with her. But there is a more subtle form of unloveliness which men find hard to forgive. It is doubly danger-ous because it creeps in unrecognized to destroy that most precious feminine quality – personal daintiness." Woodbury Soap makes a similar point, warning women that a man expects "daintiness, charm and refinement in the woman he knows, and if some unpleasant little detail mars this conception, nothing quite effaces his involuntary disappointment." Deodorants address the negative issue, perfume the positive.

Now they whisper *to* her...not *about* her

Fragrantly feminine
... SO DESIRABLE

since she uses this lovelier way to avoid offending...Since she bathes with exquisite, scented Cashmere Bouquet Soap.

"Mum" is the word!

The Alluring Charm of a Dainty Woman

ALL the attractiveness of beauty, social grace, and winning personality can be so easily set at naught by the neglect of one important attribute of feminine loveliness—personal daintiness.

It is so easy *not* to realize that one is subject to the unpleasant odor of perspiration. Almost never are you conscious of this unpleasantness yourself. And the subject is so delicate that your closest friend would not speak about it.

A simple precaution

But really careful women, women to whom complete personal attractiveness means so much, take a simple precaution that protects them *absolutely* from even the thought of an unpleasant body odor—for all day and evening.

"Mum" is the original and truly effective deodorant cream—pure white in color and easy and pleasant to use. "Mum" is applied as you dress, to the underarm and wherever perspiration is closely confined. The instant perspiration occurs, "Mum" immediately robs it of its disagreeable odor.

"Mum" is the tried, approved and safe deodorant. It has been used for years by millions of women who would not think of entrusting their personal daintiness to mere soap-and-water cleanliness nor to makeshift substitutes which give only temporary relief.

An important use

Dainty women are also grateful to "Mum" for its effectiveness when used on the sanitary napkin. In this important use "Mum" is essential to women's poise and peace of mind.

You will find "Mum" at every drug store, 25c. and 50c. (Special introductory size of "Mum" will be sent to you postpaid for 10c.)

Be sure to read our special offer, introducing to you "Amoray," the exquisitely perfumed Talc.

"Mum" prevents all body odors

Special Offer: We want you to know of "Amoray"—a new idea for the toilette of the fastidious woman. Although a talc of the finest Italian grind, astonishingly soft and smooth, "Amoray" is something more. It is perfumed by a costly process with the fragrance of many flowers from the fields of France. It is really a perfume in powder form.

In order to introduce "Amoray" to you, we shall be glad to send you a 25c jar of "Mum" and a 25c container of "Amoray"—both for 40c postpaid. The coupon is for your convenience.

"Mum" used on the foot neutralizes the *acids* of perspiration and makes silk hosiery last longer.

"MUM"
A Delicate Deodorant

THE CREATION OF BEAUTY AS AN ANCIENT & HONORED CRAFT

*M*ost of us stand in awe of skills and crafts which depend on methods and insights passed quietly from generation to generation. The Masons claim descent from those who built the Egyptian pyramids. Many liqueurs are compounded from antique recipes passed down through family members, or within a monastic order. Good cooks usually have in their repertoire one or more recipes or techniques they have received privately and guard closely. Since perfumeries also have their craft secrets, it is only natural that cosmetic manufacturers, even those without antique credentials, should try to derive power from this tradition. Palmolive Soap mined this vein most fully. Their advertisements featured lovely paintings in which a woman of today is shown with a woman of the ancient world behind her. Ancient Egypt was their favorite setting. They trans-

late a three thousand year old inscription in hieroglyphics, "as for her who desires beauty, she is wise to anoint her limbs with oil of palm and oil of olives." Palm and olive oils were the principal ingredients of Palmolive. Cleopatra, in another ad, bends over a contemporary woman and inspires her to the right use of Palmolive Soap. They remind us that "pretty girls have always known the secret." These advertisements make the modern user of the products feel that she is part of an ancient and hermetic tradition.

PALMOLIVE

Re-Incarnation of Beauty

JUST as the Egyptian Princess of 3,000 years ago bequeathed a heritage of beauty to the modern girl, so did she also hand down knowledge of the surest way to keep it.

She knew that Palm and Olive Oils were mild, beneficial, natural cleansers, as soothing in their action as a lotion. A crude combination was all she could command—today she would use *Palmolive.*

For the mild, soothing, profuse lather of Palmolive Soap, so smooth and creamy, embodies this oldest beauty secret.

Palmolive beautifies while it cleanses because it is made from the same rare oils used as both cleanser and lotion in ancient Egypt.

Palmolive is sold by leading dealers and supplied by popular hotels in guestroom size.

*Send 25c in stamps for Palmolette case
containing miniature packages of 8
favorite Palmolive requisites.*

The Palmolive Company, Milwaukee, U. S. A.
The Palmolive Company of Canada, Limited
Toronto, Ont.

PALMOLIVE

Palm Olive Shampoo

When natural resources are inadequate to the solution of our problems we frequently turn to magic. With magic we can hope to alter the seemingly inevitable course of events; even nullify the dependence of effect on cause. With its assistance one hopes to conform reality to one's desires.

Makers of beauty products frequently evoke magic. The buyers wish to erase the erosion of time, to look younger than they are, and if possible, to be even more beautiful than normal artifice allows.

The advertisers, recognizing the irrationality of the appeal to magic, additionally evoke the power of nature, promising to gain her aid in the quest for transformation.

The appeals to magic and nature's assistance are not, in most cases, directly admitted. Ours is an age of reason, and the direct statement of such claims would open them to derision. The connections are made through image, suggestion and indirection. Because reason is not directly confronted the messages slip past the guardians, and yet alter the buyer's intentions.

LE GRAND PARFUM À LA MODE

FLEURS DE MOUSSE DE SAUZÉ FRÈRES PARFUMEURS PARIS

Fleurs de Mousse, with the help of a cloud of butterflies, assist a nude woman to a state of ecstacy. Djer-Kiss (the supreme talent in this field) shows us a fairy advising a horde of elves in the capturing of a rainbow's essence so that it might be processed into various Djer-Kiss beauty products. Robertine, we discover, is not manufactured, but bottled from a green and fragrant spring that pours from a gargoyle's mouth.

The girl in the spider-web negligee seems as if she has had the help of friendly spiders in adorning herself. There occurs frequently this hint that nature conspires to help woman to her goal of beauty because of her special affinity with it. Ipswich Hosiery says that, "a witch is one who exerts powers more than natural; an irresistible influence." They also assert that, "the modern witch weaves a spell in fine, full-fashioned hosiery." This concept accords with a strong tendency to believe that women, more frequently than men, derive power from supernatural collaboration.

As a mountain climber, when he puts on his boots and gathers his climbing gear, anticipates the isolation, strain and delicious fear of the climb to come, so woman, making herself beautiful, enjoys in advance the results of her transformation.

BEAUTY PRODUCTS CREATE DESIRE IN THE USER AS WELL AS THE BEHOLDER

BEAUTY PRODUCTS CREATE DESIRE IN THE USER AS WELL AS THE BEHOLDER

Humankind needs to be taught almost every social action and response. Beauty advertising is one of the teachers of women. It instructs them not only what to fear, what to buy, and what to do with it, but also, how to be desirable, even how to desire.

BEAUTY PRODUCTS CREATE DESIRE IN THE USER AS WELL AS THE BEHOLDER

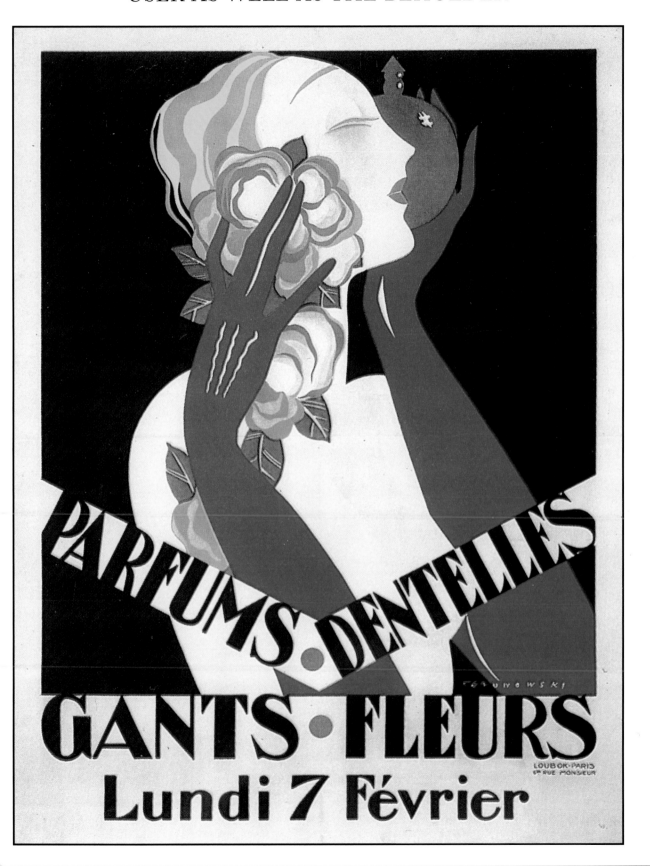

As I said in the section on the necessity of vigilance, the advertisers encourage paranoia. "You against the rest of womankind – your beauty – your charm – your skin." In the face of such a challenge some women, rather than quail before the scope of the challenge, face it squarely. They accept the idea that they are to be judged as art objects, and furthermore that the perceiving and judging is never-ending. Such women see themselves as designers, and joy in the challenge of continually recreating themselves into beautiful forms. A Kröul Toiletries brochure for 1929 bears the title *Your Masterpiece– Yourself*. It urges the reader to: "analyze yourself thoroughly. Face your problems, and then, by the use of modern cosmetics, solve your problems one by one, achieving natural loveliness. The secret of beauty lies entirely within yourself."

There is no reason that a woman cannot be creative and individualistic in her quest for beauty. She need not accept all the warnings and counsels of advertisers, but can set her own our course for the physical redefinition of herself.

Les rouges

RITZ

Pour les lèvres - Pour les joues
fleurissent la femme

ORIGINAL DESSINÉ AVEC LES PRODUITS „RITZ"

WOMEN MUST DESIGN THEMSELVES

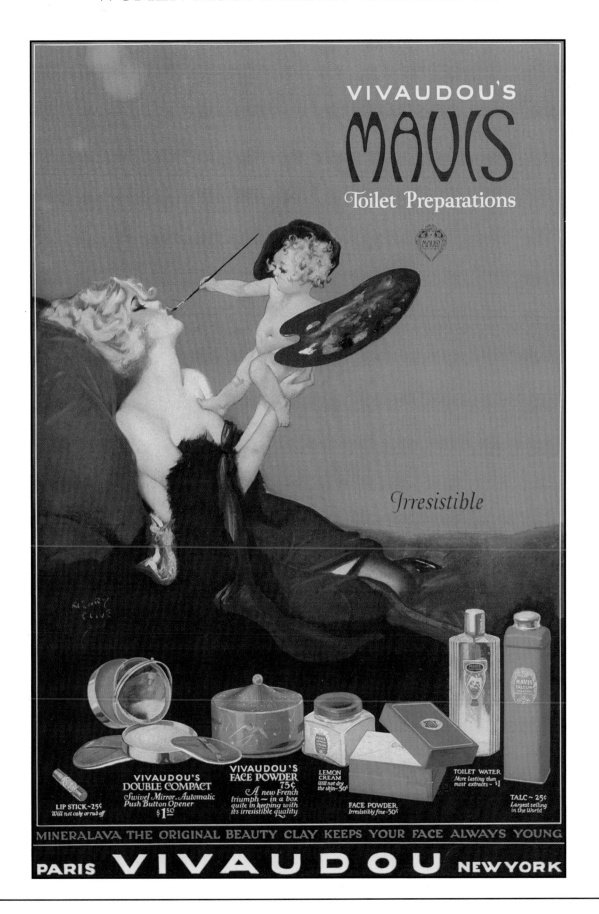

WOMEN MUST DESIGN THEMSELVES

Advertisers for beauty enhancers very frequently show women contemplating reflections of themselves. This very natural image has deep roots and long lasting consequences.

Since men, in the same periodicals, are seldom shown looking at themselves, there is the clear implication that mirror-looking is a characteristic female activity. This is the view that prevails in literature and art (for literature see Jenijoy LaBelle's *Herself Beheld*, or for art Anne Hollander's *Seeing Through Clothes*).

Mirrors reveals that which we cannot otherwise see of ourselves. It shows us how the world beholds us.

Mirror-looking jolts us out of our tendency to subjectivity, and forces on us an objective view of ourselves. It reminds us that others see us primarily as physical entities, our whole interior universe being almost invisible.

Recurrent images of mirror viewing encourages more mirror viewing in readers, and mirror viewing leads to the insecurity which is the foundation of the cosmetics industry.

*Y*our Hair Appears Twice as Beautiful—*when Shampooed this way*

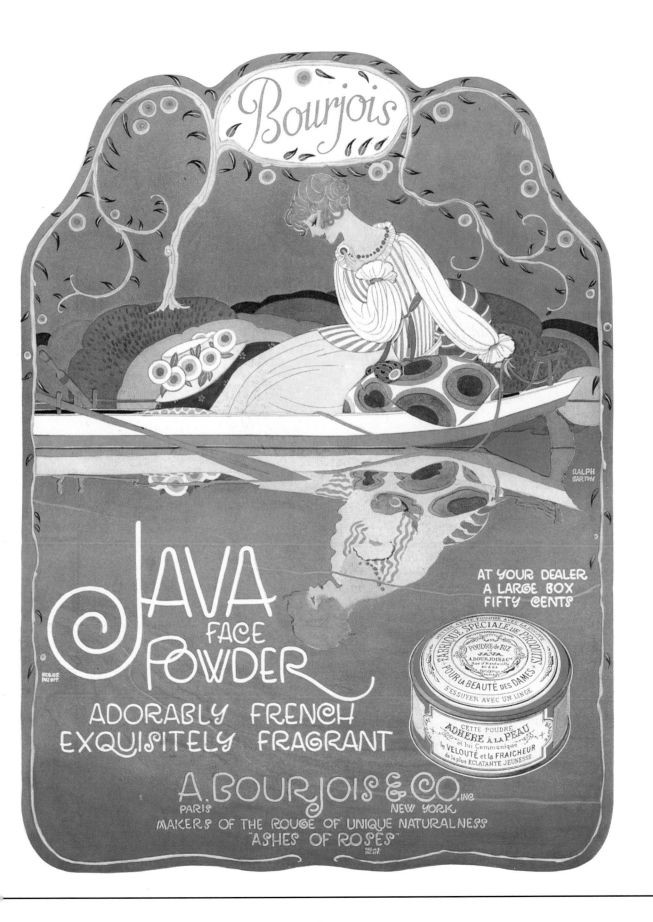

The tomb of Hathseput, the Egyptian Queen (circa 1500 b.c.) contained a lovely turquoise-blue perfume bottle. Containers for perfume, rouge, powder, body oils, pomade and coloring are routinely found in the ruins of ancient civilizations. Though glass is the most frequent material, precious metals and gemstones have also been used. A tradition of lovely containers for materials meant to promote beauty has continued throughout history. As mass production and mass marketing replaced handcraft in small quantities, the problem shifted from skilled

THE GIFT OF BEAUTY SHOULD BE
SUITABLY CONTAINED

workers and fine materials to a problem in industrial ingenuity, and the designers with their skills have created packages with their own style and goodness.

In a cedar wood chest, protected by Oriental carpets, a great number of bottles of fine glass, ornamented with gold and silver with stoppers of silver gilt or precious stones, held enclosed in their many-colored wombs all the perfumes and all the sweet scents of Araby and the Blessed. Face paints of brilliant tones and perfume paste in enchanting pots of painted earthenware or faience with lids embossed and inlaid with enamel.

— The Song of Roland

*T*he packaging of cosmetics demands attention to every element. In the more expensive products many elements are coordinated to make the desired impression. Beginning on the outside one might encounter a seal, a wrapping, a box, a container, another seal, a label. This layered richness leaves the purchaser feeling as if she were opening a casket of jewels.

The label is one of the most important of the elements, because it carries the dual burden of giving both symbolic and practical messages.

France has excelled in the design and production of perfume labels, as it has in almost all aspects of those trades relating to the adornment of woman.

Most of the labels reproduced in the following pages are French, and were created somewhere between 1900 and 1920. All of the labels

reproduced in facsimile, and enclosed in an envelope at the rear of this volume are from this golden period. They are wonderfully conceived, designed and printed, and we add them to this book to further demonstrate how superbly art has been used to make beautiful those products created for the enhancement of beauty.

Parfum Concentré de Jn GIRAUD FILS GRASSE - PARIS

Le Bouquet de Pierrot

PICARD Parfumeur
Paris.

CONTENIS 1 FL OZ.

High Life
PERFUME
ALMOR PRODUCTS CO.
H LAGO ILL U S A.

EAU
DE
COLOGNE
•
Véritable Parfum
de Fleurs

J. ARTAUD
PARIS

SAVON A LA MOUSSE DE CHÊNE
et aux Violettes des Bois

LOOK ME
OVER
REG. U.S.
PAT. OFF.
BRAND
Perfume
CONTENTS
½ OZ.

DISTRIBUTED BY
FAMOUS PRODUCTS CO
CHICAGO ILL U S A

LABELS

LES FLEURS NIÇOISES
Bruyère

Grands Magasins
de la BOURSE
BRUXELLES
Nº 405

PRINCESS PAT
EYE SHADOW

BLEND OVER UPPER LID WITH
FINGER TIP--UP TO BROW AND
DOWN TO LASHES. DARKEST
AT LASHES. APPLY LESS FOR
DAY THAN FOR EVENING.

BLUE

LOTION
EDISTA

PRÉPARÉE
PAR

A. PICARD

PARFUMEUR·CHIMISTE
34, Rue St Anne
PARIS

Un Rêve

LORENZY-PALANCA
PARIS

EAU
DE
COLOGNE

Viridiflor
FOUGÈRE

Jⁿ GIRAUD. Fils
· PARIS ·

PARFUM
BRISE
AMOUREUSE

A. PICARD
PARFUMEUR
PARIS

MADAM JONES
REG U S PAT OFF

CONTENTS   3 OUNCES

HAIR
SPARKLE
OIL

Rub on SCALP, sprinkle on
HAIR - Brush HAIR in place

DISTRIBUTED AND COPYRIGHTED 1946 BY
MADAM JONES CO.
CHICAGO, ILL. U. S. A.

PATÄNGI PERFUMES
free of alcohol
made in france

OTTO
VIOLET
CAMILLI, ALBERT & LALOUE
GRASSE FRANCE

SAVON EXTRA-PUR
ALEXANDRA
Nº 820
PARIS
AUX PARFUMS D'ORIENT

LOTION
Frimousse d'Or
LORENZY-PALANCA
PARIS

Lady Marian
TOILET WATER
Salux
Perfumer
St.Louis. USA.

L'AURÉOLE
SAVON EXTRA FIN
A LA VIOLETTE
SAVONNERIE P. TRANOY
TOURCOING
Nº 335

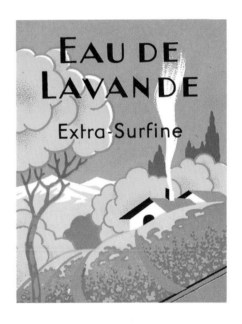

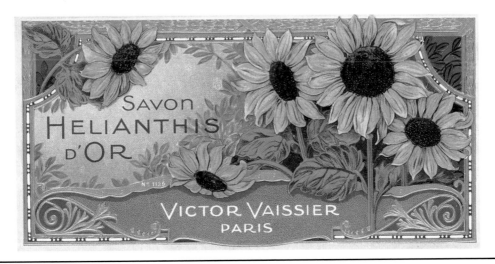

Cover	**F.A.S.** Trilety's Toiletries advertisement, n.d.
Half-title	**Pressler, Gene.** Pussywillow Face Powder advertisement, n.d.
Frontispiece	**Anonymous.** Mavis Cosmetics advertisement, 1919
Title page	**Anonymous.** Holeproof Hosiery advertisement, n.d.
© page	**Barbier, George.** *The Romance of Perfume*, 1928
1	**Anonymous.** Palmolive Soap advertisement, 1926
2	**J.A.** Coty Perfume advertisement, 1937
3	**Anonymous.** Camay Soap advertisement, 1933
4	**Pressler, Gene.** Pompeian Beauty Powder advertisement, 1922
5	**Anonymous.** Old South Toiletries advertisement, 1946
6	Top: **Anonymous.** Dove Complexion Powder advertisement, n.d.
	Bottom: **Anonymous.** Palmolive Soap advertisement, 1928
7	**Anonymous.** Palmolive Soap advertisement, 1922
8	**Andersen, M.** Azurea Perfume advertisement, 1924
9	**Woodbury, M.C.** McCallum Hosiery advertisement, 1921
10	**Christy, Earl.** Watkins Shampoo advertisement, 1926
11	**L.L.L.** Palmolive Soap advertisement, 1926
12	**Anonymous.** Cashmere Bouquet Soap advertisement, 1936
13	**C.B.C.** Mum Deodorant advertisement, 1927
14	**Anonymous.** Fine Art Toilet Soap advertisement, n.d.
15	**McMein.** Palmolive Soap advertisement, n.d.
16	**Metlicovitz, Leopoldo.** French perfume advertisement, 1906
17	**Richardson, F.** Djer-Kiss cosmetics advertisement, 1920
18	Top left: **Anonymous.** Florida Water advertisement, 1880
	Top right: **Anonymous.** Wisdom's Robertine Soap advertisement, 1887
	Bottom: **Anonymous.** Persian Bouquet Perfume advertisement, n.d.
19	**Phillips, Coles.** Holeproof Hosiery advertisement, 1921
20	**Loupot, Charles.** Coty Lipstick advertisement, 1938
21	**Metlicovitz, Leopoldo.** Flouvella Perfume advertisement, n.d.
22	**Anonymous.** Linit Soap advertisement, n.d.
23	**Gronowski, Tadeusz.** *Parfums • Dentelles • Gants • Fleurs*, 1927
24	Top: **Phillips, Coles.** Gainsborough cosmetics advertisement, 1923
	Bottom: **Orsi.** Les Rouges Ritz advertisement, 1928
25	**Clive, Henry.** Vivaudou cosmetics advertisement, 1923
26	**Christy, Earl.** Watkins Shampoo advertisement, 1926
27	**Barton, Ralph.** Java Face Powder cosmetics advertisement, n.d.
28	**Anonymous.** Rigaud Perfume advertisement, 1919
29	Top: **Anonymous.** Nylotis Talcum Powder advertisement, 1914
	Bottom: **Anonymous.** Le Jade Perfume advertisement, n.d.
30-35	Assorted perfume labels appear on these pages.
Endpapers	Assorted perfume labels.
Back cover	**Anonymous.** Pears' Soap advertisement, n.d.